Whiskers
&
Rhymes

Whiskers & Rhymes

WRITTEN AND ILLUSTRATED BY

Arnold Lobel

GREENWILLOW BOOKS, NEW YORK

Library of Congress Cataloging in Publication Data

Lobel, Arnold.   Whiskers and rhymes.
Summary: A collection of short humorous
poems in the nursery rhyme tradition.
1. Children's poetry, American. [1. Humorous poetry.
2. Nursery rhymes. 3. American poetry] I. Title.
PS3562.018W45 1985   811'.54   83-25424
ISBN 0-688-03835-2
ISBN 0-688-03836-0 (lib. bdg.)

For Orson

CONTENTS

Sing, sing, what shall we sing?
A song to delight your ear.
Sing, sing, how shall we sing?
With a sound that is loud and clear.

Strum, strum, when shall we strum?
As we carry our fine guitars.
Strum, strum, where shall we strum?
By your window, under the stars.

9

Sing a song of succotash,
A bucketful of noses.
And here is one for each of you,
To help you sniff the roses.

Boom, boom!
My feet are large.
Each shoe is like a garbage barge.
Boom, boom!
My poor head aches.
Wherever I step, the sidewalk breaks.

Little pictures
Hang above me.
Pictures of the folks
Who love me.
Mom and Dad
And Uncle Jack,
They love me . . .
I love them back.

Although he didn't like the taste,
George brushed his teeth with pickle paste.
Not ever was his mouth so clean,
Not ever were his teeth so green.

Whiskers of style,
Whiskers of grace,
Whiskers that grow
On the sides of my face.
I went to the barber
To ask of him,
"Please give these whiskers
A handsome trim."
He sharpened his scissors,
But I'm sad to report,
He cut each whisker
A mile too short.

Orson Porson,
Pudding and pie,
He ran away
And made me cry.
Orson Porson,
Knotty pine,
He came back
And I feel fine.

It rains and it pours.
I've got too many chores,
There's the cooking and cleaning to do.
I'd rather be out on a wet, green hill,
Laughing and dancing with you.

Clara, little curlylocks,
Went out among the trees and rocks.
She met a lion in his lair,
Which gave that girl an awful scare.
Her sudden fear was so intense . . .
Those curls stood up like a picket fence.

18

Loose and limber,
Beanbag Jim
Seems to have
No bones in him.
At carnivals
And vaudeville shows
He ties himself
In knots and bows.
He's known to all
Throughout the land
As nature's living
rubber band.

Sakes alive!
It's almost five!
It's time to have my dinner.
The outer part of me is fine,
But what about my inner?

Mirror, mirror, over the sink,
What do you see when I take a drink?
One nose, one mouth, two eyes that blink.
How you'd love this face if you could think!

Two brothers are we,
Two gloomy men.
Our clock has lost its chime.
We ought to wind it up again,
But we can't find the time.

Old Tom, he was a merry one,
A merry one was he.
He took a cup and filled it up
With gingerberry tea.
Old Tom, he was a dizzy one,
A dizzy one was he.
He bumped his head and went to bed
At quarter after three.

I married a wife on Sunday.
She cooked a wedding stew.

I felt so sick on Monday,
She asked what she should do.

Upon my bed on Tuesday,
I still was feeling ill.

No better yet on Wednesday,
She made me take a pill.

I asked for food on Thursday,
She fed me buttered bread.

I felt so well on Friday,
I jumped right out of bed.

Full health returned on Saturday.
I cried, "Enough of this!"

When morning came on Sunday,
I gave my bride a kiss.

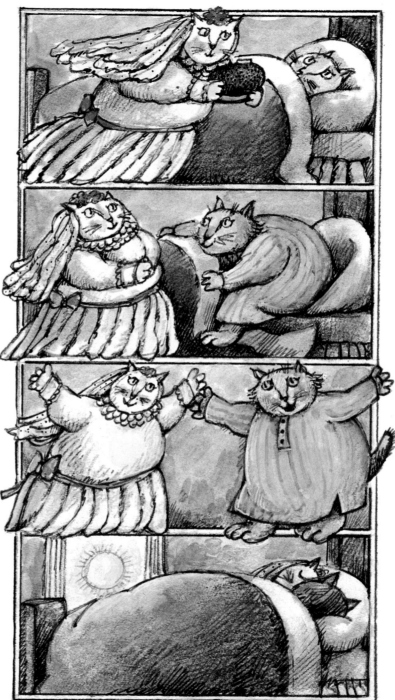

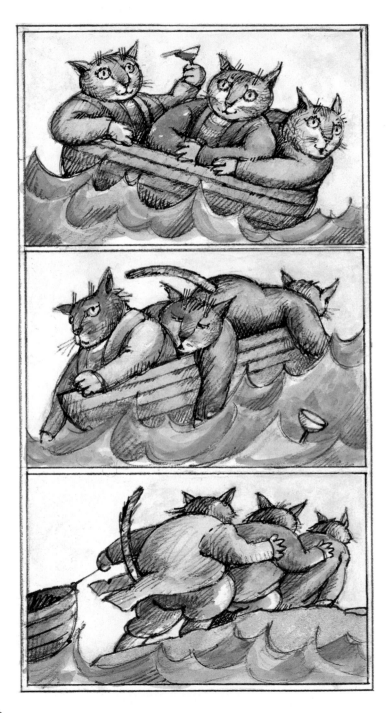

Gaily afloat,
Three men in a boat,
In the sun on the waves of the ocean.
But their faces got burned
And their stomachs were turned
By the rollicking, frolicking motion.

She listens to the waves resound,
She gazes at the sea.
I wish that she would turn around
And simply smile at me.

There was a man
Dressed all in cheese.
Certain was he
That the sight would please.
Though his neighbors agreed,
Those clothes looked well on him,
They ran far away
From that certain smell on him.

Trouble, oh trouble,
My temper is lost.
I always see double
When my eyes are crossed.

Books to the ceiling, books to the sky.
My piles of books are a mile high.
How I love them! How I need them!
I'll have a long beard by the time I read them.

There was a messy gentleman
Who lived a sloppy life.
He ate with dirty forks and spoons,
And never washed a knife.
The pattern on his tablecloth
Was proof of his disorder,
For ketchup made the polka dots,
And mustard made the border.

Tired old peddler,
        how he sags,
From hauling safety pins in bags.
And heavy, heavy on his back,
The weight of toothpicks in a sack.

My London Bridge
Has just one task,
It has to stand . . .
That's all I ask.
It has to stand
And that is all,
It may not bend
Or break or fall.

My London Bridge
Has just one task,
It has to stand . . .
That's all I ask.
It has to stand
And nothing more,
To let me cross
From shore to shore.

My London Bridge
Has just one task,
It has to stand . . .
That's all I ask.
It has to stand
And not forget
To keep my shoes
From getting wet.

Andrew was an apple thief.
He stole the pears
    and cherries.
He pushed aside
    each vine and leaf
To grab the grapes
    and berries.
One night,
    while pilfering a peach,
This life of crime he quit.
He snatched that fruit,
His final reach . . .
And choked upon the pit.

Sleeping Charlie in his chair,
Feathered wings have sprouted there.
Away flies Charlie, through the air,
Across the skies to everywhere.

Twinkle Toes,
He comes and goes,
In and out the door.
He can't remember
Where he's been
A minute or so before.

Polly Barlor, in the parlor,
Doing the trickiest things.
For while chewing some gum,
She nibbled her thumb,
And pulled out the stickiest strings.

I will give you the key
To this garden gate.
Bright summer
Lives over the wall.
You may play in the sun
Till the season grows late,
And bring back the key in the fall.

If you were a pot
And I were a pan,
We could sit on the shelf together.
If you were a mountain
And I were the snow,
We wouldn't much mind the weather.

Mistress Pratt,

Round and fat,

By accident sat

Upon her hat.

She squashed it flat

And that was that.

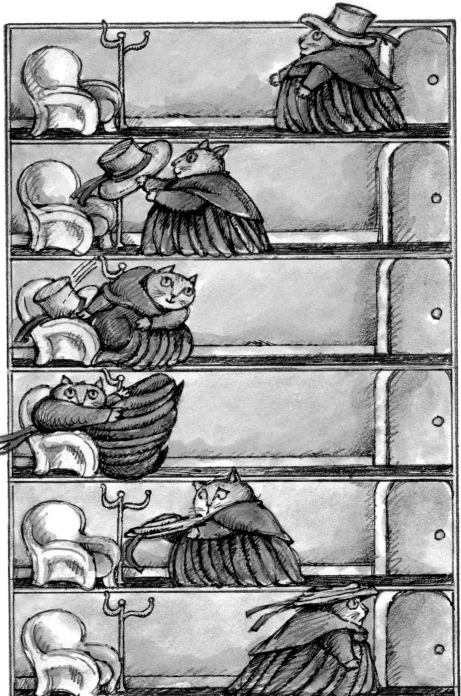

Friendly Fredrick Fuddlestone
Could fiddle on his funny bone.
When Freddy fiddled
    foolishly fast,
He found his father
    frankly aghast.
Friendly Fredrick Fuddlestone
Kept fiddling on his funny bone.
His furious father
    would flatly forbid it,
Which, of course,
    is why young Freddy did it.

Postman, postman,
Ring my bell.
You are here
And all is well.
Postman, postman,
Bring my mail.
Let me serve you
Cakes and ale.
The day was sad,
But now it's better . . .
A friend has written me a letter.

Vain, vain, Mister McLain,
Dressed in his best suit and vest.
He was caught in the rain
As he strolled down the lane,
And became very quickly unpressed.

There was an old woman of long ago
Who went about her mending.
She sewed the wind against the clouds
To stop the trees from bending.
She stitched the sun to the highest hill
To hold the day from ending.

Her thimble and threads were close at hand
For needlework and quilting,
For sewing gardens to the sky
To keep the blooms from wilting,
For lacing the land to the crescent moon
To save the world from tilting.

This lamp in my window
Glows warmly, shines bright.
It guides friends and strangers
Who travel at night.